RAND

Operation Just Cause

Lessons for Operations Other Than War

Jennifer Morrison Taw

Prepared for the
United States Army

Arroyo Center

Approved for public release; distribution unlimited

Contents

Preface iii

Summary. vii

Acknowledgments xi

Abbreviations xiii

1.   INTRODUCTION   1

2.   OPERATION JUST CAUSE   3
     Background   3
     Operation Just Cause   6

3.   OPERATIONAL DIMENSIONS   9
     Command Relationships   9
     Planning   10
     Force Structure   12
     Coordination Between the Players   14
     Training   16
     Intelligence   17
     Logistics   19
     Equipment   20
     Military Operations on Urban Terrain   22
     Rules of Engagement and Collateral Damage   24
     Stability Operations   26
     Postconflict Military Operations   27

4.   RECOMMENDATIONS FOR THE ARMY   30
     Joint Planning   30
     Force Structure   30
     Coordination   31
     Training   31
     Intelligence   32
     Equipment   32
     Postcombat Operations   33
     Conclusion   34

Appendix: TASK FORCE ORGANIZATION   35

Bibliography   37

Summary

A superpower whipped the poop out of 10 percent of the police force of a Third World nation. You are supposed to be able to do that. It was done well, and I credit those who did it. But it is important that we draw the right lessons from it.

—anonymous U.S. Marine[1]

Operation Just Cause (OJC) was an operationally successful contingency operation. But it should have been. During its course, the United States arrayed 26,000 men and women of the U.S. armed forces—13,000 of whom were already stationed in Panama and were familiar with its terrain, military, government, and people—against the 15,000-man security force of the Panamanian Defense Forces (PDF), of which only 3,500 were soldiers. The Panamanian military was no mystery to the U.S. forces, who had conducted extensive training of the PDF and were well versed in its doctrine, training, and capabilities. Nor did the U.S. military face any angry crowds, violent uprisings, or even passive popular resistance: the people of Panama welcomed the Americans and provided little, if any, support to the PDF. Communication with the PDF and the public was not a serious problem, because many members of the U.S. military speak Spanish as a first or second language. Finally, tension between the United States and Panama mounted for more than a year, allowing sufficient time for planning and practicing an operation such as Just Cause. Each of these factors contributed to the ease and speed with which the PDF was defeated and U.S. military objectives were successfully met.

Without these unique advantages, however, OJC could have been much more devastating and could have required a much longer-term U.S. commitment. Posit, for example, the effects on such an operation of a more hostile population in a less familiar country, such as is likely to take place in the future: Had the U.S. forces faced stiffer PDF resistance in Panama City, for example, they would probably have found that they had received inadequate preparation and training for military operations on urban terrain (MOUT). Had U.S. forces encountered violent or even passive civilian opposition to the invasion, they could have found

---

[1]"Some Question Whether the U.S. Is Ready for LIC," *Navy News and Undersea Technology*, 27 August 1990, p. 7.

themselves involved in an unconventional urban conflict requiring manpower they did not have and riot control, MOUT, and counterinsurgency operations for which they were neither trained or prepared. Had the operation taken place where the local people spoke an African, Southeast Asian, or other dialect (or dialects), the famous "Ma Bell" approach (wherein U.S. forces called barricaded PDF forces and offered them the opportunity to surrender) could not have been so widely used, and other highly effective civil affairs and PSYOP operations would have been severely constrained by both language difficulties and overall unfamiliarity with the locale. Had U.S. forces been less familiar with the terrain, or had fewer opportunities to train in the area, the problems getting accurate maps and unit-appropriate intelligence preparation of the battlefield (IPB) would have been more serious. Even with U.S. forces' knowledge of the country, the invasion was slowed when heavy-drop platforms (including Sheridan tanks) were accidentally parachuted into a bog and, in another incident, parachutists were dropped into tall grass away from their designated drop zone.[2] Finally, if half the U.S. forces involved in the operation were not already in place, some of the U.S. sealift and airlift shortfalls noted in Operation Desert Storm might have affected OJC, and logistics and timing would have been much more complicated than they were.

Also, because OJC was a unilateral effort, no coalition issues or problems complicated or slowed U.S. operations. The communications, logistics, planning, and command-and-control issues that arise in multinational operations never arose during OJC. Nor did the United States have to coordinate its efforts with nongovernmental organizations (NGOs) or humanitarian relief organizations (HROs). Yet, as recent events attest, future U.S. operations other than war (OOTW) are unlikely to be unilateral. As much as they benefited from both coalition and NGO/HRO cooperation, operations in Somalia, Rwanda, and Haiti demonstrate that U.S. forces will also have to adjust training and doctrine to accommodate such combined efforts.[3]

OJC could thus almost be considered fortunate. It afforded the United States the opportunity to conduct a conventional contingency operation with some of the key characteristics of OOTW under extremely advantageous circumstances. The

---

[2]Terry White, *Swords of Lightning: Special Forces and the Changing Face of Warfare*, London: Brassey's (UK), 1992, p. 260.

[3]This monograph does not address military responses to the media's role in military OOTW or in OJC specifically. For some discussion of the role of the media, please see J. E. Crichton, *Department of Defense Press Pool: Did It Work in Panama*, Master's Thesis, Tucson, AZ: The University of Arizona, 1990; P. L. Aswell, *Wartime Press Censorship by the U.S. Armed Forces: A Historical Perspective*, Master's Thesis, Fort Leavenworth, KS: U.S. Army Command and General Staff College, 1990, pp. 129–146; and J. R. Vallance-Whitacre, *An Evaluation of the Media Coverage Concerning the Mission to Secure the Dog Kennel During the Panama Invasion on December 20, 1989*, Master's Thesis, Richmond, VA: Virginia Commonwealth University, 1990.

errors and miscues that did take place were to be expected: OJC represented a significant departure from either the battlefield warfare for which U.S. forces have trained since the end of World War II or the unconventional jungle operations of the Vietnam War. Planning and operations were fully integrated across all four services; much of the operation was conducted on urban terrain; a large number (the largest number since Vietnam, but surpassed during ODS) of U.S.-based forces were rapidly deployed; special operations forces played a highly visible and crucial role in the operation; rules of engagement were uncommonly restrictive; soldiers were expected to apply minimum use of force; indirect fire and aerial bombing were limited; surgical strikes were necessary; and a key objective was the preservation and defense of infrastructure and public utilities.

These characteristics are also common to recent operations other than war (especially "peace operations" and humanitarian assistance) in Somalia, Bosnia, Iraq (among the Kurds), Bangladesh, Rwanda, and Haiti. Despite OJC's unique advantages, the U.S. Army can draw practical lessons from the operation for application in current and future OOTW:

- Army training in MOUT remains inadequate, and more units should include MOUT in their mission essential task lists (METLs).

- Intelligence remains an issue as well; electronic intelligence is insufficient in OOTW, and must be supplemented by human intelligence and imagery. Just Cause demonstrated a need for improved interagency coordination for sharing and disseminating intelligence, especially HUMINT. While interagency coordination on intelligence still proved problematic in Operation Desert Storm, by the time of Operations Provide Relief and Restore Hope in Somalia, the situation had somewhat improved.

- More generally, efforts to streamline joint operations must not overlook service-specific needs, and must maintain particular care to maximize use of special operations forces by employing them in the specialized tasks for which they were trained.

- Equipment was also an issue in OJC, and the special requirements of MOUT were clearly demonstrated. Advancements in technology applicable to OOTW have been made since 1989, but the military's priority in research and development remains on conventional weaponry and materiel.

- Planning for OOTW must not overlook or underemphasize stability operations, as was done in OJC. If the traditional process of assigning planning responsibilities for combat and noncombat operations to disparate organizations is continued, sufficient coordination must take place.

Abbreviations

ABN	Airborne
ACC	Air Component Command
AR	Armor
AVN	Aviation
BDE	Brigade
BN	Battalion
BTTY	Battery
CAB	Civil affairs battalion
CALL	Center for Army Lessons Learned
CATF	Civil Affairs Task Force
CINC	Commander in chief
CMOTF	Civil Military Operations Task Force
CO	Company
COMJTF-SO	Commander, Joint Task Force *South*
CRE	Combat readiness exercise
CSS	Combat service support
CTC	Combat training center
DET	Detachment
DIGBAT	Dignity battalion
ELINT	Electronic intelligence
FAO	Foreign area officer
FLIR	Forward looking infrared
GOP	Government of Panama
GP	Group
HB TM	Loudspeaker team
HMMWV	High mobility multipurpose vehicle
HRO	Humanitarian relief organization
HUMINT	Human intelligence
ICITAP	International Criminal Investigation Training Assistance Program

ID	Infantry Division
IFF	Identification, friend or foe
IMINT	Imagery intelligence
INF	Infantry
IPB	Intelligence preparation of the battlefield
JCS	Joint Chiefs of Staff
JPOTF	Joint Psychological Operations Task Force
JSOTF	Joint Special Operations Task Force
JTF	Joint task force
JTFSO	Joint Task Force *South*
LAW	Light antitank weapon
LO	Liaison officer
LT	Light
MAC	Military Airlift Command
MECH	Mechanized infantry
METL	Mission essential task list
MOUT	Military operations on urban terrain
MP	Military Police
MSG	Military Support Group
NEO	Noncombatant evacuation operation
NGO	Nongovernmental organization
NOTAR	NO Tail Rotor
NSWG	Naval special warfare group
NSWU	Naval special warfare unit
NVG	Night vision goggles
ODS	Operation Desert Storm
OFLD	Public Force Liaison Division
OJC	Operation Just Cause
OOTW	Operations other than war
OPLAN	Operation plan
OPORD	Operation order
ORH	Operation Restore Hope
PDF	Panamanian Defense Forces
PLT	Platoon

PNP	Panamanian National Police
POG	Psychological operations group
PSYOP	Psychological operations
REGT	Regiment
RGR	Ranger
ROE	Rules of engagement
SEAL	Sea-Air-Land
SF	Special forces
SFGA	Special forces group, airborne
SMU	Special marine unit
SOAG	Special operations aviation group
SOF	Special Operations Forces
SOP	Standard operating procedure
SOUTHCOM	Southern Command
SOW	Special operations wing
STX	Situational training exercise
SWAT	Special weapons and tactics units
TAC	Tactical Air Command
TADS/PNVS	Target Acquisition Designation Sight/Pilot Night Vision Sensor
TF	Task force
USARSO	United States Army South
USCINCSO	United States Commander-in-Chief South
USFLG	United States Foreign Liaison Group
USSOCOM	United States Special Operations Command

troops were already based in Panama and had conducted regular exercises there. The U.S. government and military had both enjoyed long and cooperative relationships with Panamanian government and military leaders. And the U.S. invasion of Panama was a unilateral action, based strictly on U.S. interests, and is unlikely to be repeated in this post–Cold War era of collective engagement and combined operations (often conducted under the aegis of the United Nations). Nonetheless, despite these singular characteristics, a number of lessons for the U.S. Army can be drawn from OJC for application in future operations other than war (especially "peace operations" and humanitarian assistance efforts) as well as more conventional lesser regional contingencies.

This case study examines various aspects of OJC, identifies and discusses lessons learned, and presents possible implications for future U.S. Army military operations other than war. Among the issues considered are: U.S. military responses to the dense civilian population and the fragile urban infrastructure in Panama City; the effectiveness of U.S. force structure, deployment, coordination, logistics, and communications in this kind of conflict; the U.S. military's preparedness for military operations on urban terrain (MOUT); the rules of engagement; the role and effectiveness of civic action efforts; and postconflict military operations.

This monograph is divided into four sections and an appendix: the next section briefly examines the sequence of events leading up to and during OJC. The third section describes and assesses specific aspects of the operation. The fourth section offers recommendations for the Army. Finally, the appendix itemizes the forces and task forces involved in the operation.

2. Operation Just Cause

Nineteen months after Operation Just Cause, Panama is free, and democracy, I believe, is irreversible. The government chosen in an election [that] General Noriega tried to hijack is now in office. A free, critical press operates without fear of intimidation. Open, vigorous competition among democratic political parties has replaced the repression of the Noriega era.

—Bernard W. Aronson, Assistant Secretary for Inter-American Affairs

Background

On 6 June 1987, one of Panama leader Manuel Noriega's former associates, Colonel Roberto Diaz Herrera, gave an interview to the Panamanian press in which he described how he and Noriega had fixed the 1984 election and how they later forced President Nicolas Barletta to resign in favor of Noriega associate Eric Arturo "Tuturo" Delvalle. Within three weeks of Diaz Herrera's statement, the U.S. Senate passed by a large margin a resolution demanding that Noriega step down while the charges against him were investigated. Noriega responded by instigating an anti-American campaign that culminated in a July 1987 attack on the U.S. embassy and consular buildings in Panama City.[1]

Relations between the formerly friendly United States and Panama crossed a new threshold. The U.S. State Department billed the Panamanian government $106,000 for the damage caused during the attack on the embassy. Elliot Abrams, the Assistant Secretary of State for Inter-American affairs and a former Noriega supporter, then called on Noriega to prohibit PDF involvement in Panamanian domestic politics and to eliminate even the slightest appearance of corruption. Though not an indictment, the speech was nonetheless hailed as the harshest criticism of Noriega yet made by a U.S. government official. This was followed in September by the U.S. Senate's resolution calling for an economic and military boycott of Panama, resulting in the suspension of U.S. military and economic aid to the country. Then, in October and November 1987, the House and Senate Foreign Relations Committee each voted to cut all but humanitarian aid to

---

[1]Michele Labrut, "U.S. Facilities Stoned in Panama," *Miami Herald*, 1 July 1987.

Panama.[2] By the end of November, the U.S. Department of Defense, under congressional pressure, had cancelled two large military exercises scheduled to be held with Panama during 1988. One month later, Noriega responded by reneging on a plan for stepping down from power that had been devised in cooperation with the United States.

In January 1988, U.S. pressure against Noriega took a new turn as charges that he had directly profited from drug trafficking were made public. U.S. Assistant Secretary of Defense Richard Armitage traveled to Panama again to urge Noriega to resign from his position.[3] A week later, U.S. Secretary of State George Shultz repeated Armitage's request, publicly calling for General Noriega to "step back" from power. Then, on 4 February 1988, an American grand jury indicted Noriega on thirteen counts of narcotics trafficking and racketeering.

The United States, meanwhile, intensified its pressure on President Delvalle to remove Noriega from office—as he had often promised to do in the event that Noriega was charged with drug offenses. The Panamanian president first tried to persuade Noriega to step down of his own accord, arguing that the leader of the PDF should not be tainted with such charges. When Noriega refused, Delvalle fired him, inspiring a massive public demonstration in support of the move. The PDF dispersed crowds with tear gas, and Noriega shut down the press. Within eight hours of Delvalle's announcement, the Panamanian national assembly had voted to replace Delvalle with Manuel Solis Palma, the education minister.

The United States now pledged its support to the deposed president but took no formal action against Noriega. As "president-in-hiding," Delvalle issued a proclamation freezing all Panamanian assets outside the country. The United States cooperated by freezing $50 million in Panamanian assets and ordering the nonpayment of canal revenues and local taxes by American companies in Panama. This action, more than any, dealt a severe blow to the Panamanian economy, forcing the entire banking system to shut down for lack of U.S. currency.[4] In addition, U.S. troops—mostly military police trained in antiriot

---

[2]The suspension of aid, however, was mostly symbolic: the United States that year had already given Panama $26 million in economic aid and $6 million in military aid. Moreover, no attempt was made to reduce, much less eliminate, the Reagan administration's request for $33 million in additional military assistance to Panama for the new fiscal year. Kevin Buckley, *Panama: The Whole Story*, New York: Simon and Schuster, 1991, pp. 90–91.

[3]Elaine Sciolino, "U.S. Is Considering Action on Panama," *The New York Times*, 9 January 1988; David B. Ottoway, "Pentagon Aide Reportedly Pressures Noriega to Resign," *Los Angeles Times*, 8 January 1988.

[4]Steven Erlanger, "U.S. Economic Warfare Brings Disaster to Panama," *The New York Times*, 9 June 1988.

techniques—were dispatched to Panama in support of U.S. troops stationed there.[5]

In April 1988, the State Department reassured a concerned Noriega that the United States would not intervene militarily and began negotiating anew to drop the grand jury indictments against him provided Noriega stepped down as commander-in-chief. This course of action was contested within the U.S. government, however, where a bipartisan congressional coalition opposed dealing with Noriega. As the policymakers wrangled over their approach to the dictator, the U.S. military stepped up psychological operations (PSYOP) within Panama in an attempt to exploit perceived "restiveness" within the Panamanian Defense Forces. In May, U.S. negotiations with Noriega broke down.

Three months later, the Panamanian press reported U.S. covert plans to destabilize Noriega's regime. In fact, President Reagan had authorized a "finding" in July requesting that the CIA develop a covert strategy to oust Noriega, although it was not implemented.[6] Six months later, however, in February 1989, President Bush approved another covert action, making $10 million available to Noriega's political opponents for the May 1989 elections.[7] When violence followed Noriega's annulment of those elections after his opponents were voted into office, the United States sent yet more troops to Panama.[8]

In August 1989, President Bush again intensified the pressure against Noriega. As U.S. troops began conducting a series of highly visible military exercises in Panama, Bush let it be known that he was considering the full range of military options. He publicly urged Noriega to step down,[9] suggesting that were Noriega to leave Panama for exile in a country that barred extradition to the U.S., the United States would drop the drug-trafficking charges against him.[10] Four days later, an increasingly frustrated Bush called on the Panamanian people to oust Noriega themselves.

When Delvalle's official tenure as Panama's president ended in September 1989, the Panamanian Council of State, in a move that was considered a blatant snub of

---

[5]*Risk Assessment Monthly*, Vol. 10, No. 3, March 1988; *Risk Assessment Weekly*, Vol. 5, No. 11, 18 March 1988.

[6]Steven C. Ropp, "Panama's Defiant Noriega," *Current History*, December 1988, p. 419; Doyle McManus, "Noriega Move to End Panama Crisis Reported," *Los Angeles Times*, 5 August 1988.

[7]Lindsay Gruson, "Carter Says Soldiers Seize Tallies and Block Counting of Vote in Panama," *The New York Times*, 8 May 1989.

[8]Richard Halloran, "U.S. Troops to Go Slowly Into Panama," *The New York Times*, 12 May 1989.

[9]James Gerstenzang and John M. Broder, "Step Down, Bush Urges Noriega," *Los Angeles Times*, 10 May 1989.

[10]James Gerstenzang, "Bush Urges Coup to Topple Noriega," *Los Angeles Times*, 14 May 1989.

battalion task force (TF *Gator*), led by M-113 armored personnel carriers, attacked and cleared the Comandancia.[19]

In all, 314 PDF soldiers were killed, 124 were wounded, and 5,313 were detained. U.S. forces captured, discovered, or were given 72,000 weapons, and they seized 33 armored vehicles.[20] U.S. troops served with courage and distinction.

---

[19]Some sources identify Fort Polk's 4-6th Infantry as part of TF *Bayonet* rather than TF *Gator* (which they do not mention at all), and posit that the seizure of the Comandancia was part of TF *Bayonet*'s mission. Donna Miles, "Panama: Operation Just Cause," *Soldiers*, February 1990, p. 22.

[20]Ibid., p. 24.

3. Operational Dimensions

Operation Just Cause's mission was

- To protect American lives
- To assist the democratically elected government
- To seize and arrest an indicted drug trafficker
- To defend the integrity of U.S. rights under the canal treaties.[1]

The operational intent was to achieve this mission by presenting the PDF with overwhelming combat power in an effort to secure their surrender or terminate the combat in the shortest time possible with the least possible number of casualties on both sides and absolute minimum collateral damage.[2]

It is instructive to examine what was done to ensure the success of this operation and the fulfillment of the above mission. Moreover, such an exercise can facilitate a constructive comparison of Operation Just Cause with ongoing and future military operations other than war. By exploring such elements of the operation as planning, logistics, force structure, and postconflict efforts, lessons can be gleaned from Just Cause for application to other conflicts.

Command Relationships

The command structure for Operation Just Cause was very straightforward. At the head, following the President, was General Maxwell Thurman, Commander in Chief, U.S. Southern Command (CINCSO), with Lieutenant General Carl Stiner, the commander of Joint Task Force South (COMJTF-SO), directly beneath him. Lieutenant General Stiner, the commanding general of the XVIII Airborne Corps, had operational control of the entire fighting force, simplifying the chain of command significantly. Under his command were four conventional task forces (TF *Semper Fi*, TF *Atlantic*, TF *Pacific*, and TF *Bayonet*), the COMJTF-SO Air Component Command (ACC), and the Joint Special Operations Task Force (JSOTF). The JSOTF controlled six additional task forces (TF *Red*, TF *Green*, TF

---

[1]Excerpted speech by U.S. Secretary of State James Baker, 20 December 1989, *Latin American Weekly Report*, WR-90-1, 11 January 1990, p. 2.

[2]U.S. Special Operations Command briefing, *Operation Just Cause*, January 1990.

Black, TF *Gator*, TF *Blue*, and TF *White*) and, with the COMJTF-SO ACC, jointly controlled the JSOTF ACC. The JSOTF ACC, in turn, controlled the various air components of the operation, including the tactical air forces (TAC), the military airlift forces (MAC), the 1st Special Operations Wing (SOW), and the 160th Special Operations Aviation Group (SOAG).[3]

Planning

The United States began planning for the operation in Panama in February and March 1988, when the ELABORATE MAZE operation order (88-2) was developed from a previous, much less hostile plan. The new five-phase plan encompassed defensive operations within the old canal zone, a buildup of augmentation forces, offensive operations to neutralize the PDF, noncombatant evacuation operations (NEO), and civil-military operations to stabilize the situation and restore law and order.[4] Planning for the various phases fell, as usual, to different groups: Southern Command (SOUTHCOM) maintained control over the civil-military and stability operations OPORDs,[5] the Joint Special Operations Task Force (JSOTF) controlled special operations, and Joint Task Force (JTF) *Panama* was given responsibility for planning conventional operations within BLUE SPOON.

In June 1988, USCINCSO set up the Joint Task Force *South* (JTFSO) as the headquarters responsible for executing BLUE SPOON,[6] and LTG Carl Stiner, commander of the XVIII Airborne Corps, was designated JTFSO's commander.[7]

Nearly a year later, following the May 1989 Panamanian elections, the United States executed Operation NIMROD DANCER, augmenting the U.S. forces in Panama with a brigade headquarters and mechanized infantry. Reinforcement of forward-deployed forces then continued with Operation NIMROD SUSTAIN

---

[3]The U.S. Army South (USARSO) JTF *Panama*, which served as the Joint Task Force Headquarters in Panama until Operation Just Cause, was absorbed completely by JTF *South*.

[4]U.S. Southern Command, *Command Briefing on Operation Just Cause*, Tampa, FL: MacDill Air Force Base, USSOCOM, no date, p. 8; U.S. Special Operations Command briefing, *Operation Just Cause: Joint Special Operations Task Force (JSOTF)*, January 1990; *Operation Just Cause Lessons Learned*, Vol. 1, "Soldiers and Leadership," Fort Leavenworth, KS: Center for Army Lessons Learned (CALL), U.S. Army Combined Arms Command (CAC), October 1990, p. I-4. ELABORATE MAZE was broken down into five phases, with independent OPORDS. The OPORD for defensive operations was named ELDER STATESMAN (later changed to POST TIME); stability operations were named KRYSTAL BALL (later changed to BLIND LOGIC); noncombatant evacuation operations were named KLONDIKE KEY; defense of U.S. sites was named SECURITY ENHANCEMENT; and, of course, the OPORD for offensive operations was BLUE SPOON.

[5]SOUTHCOM set up the Civil-Military Operations Task Force (CMOTF), which had some difficulties later on coordinating with the Joint Task Force *South*.

[6]Lawrence A. Yates, "Joint Task Force Panama: JUST CAUSE—Before and After," *Military Review*, October 1991, p. 60.

[7]U.S. Southern Command, *Command Briefing on Operation Just Cause*, p. 8.

while military dependents began returning to the United States under Operation BLADE JEWEL. After the failed coup attempt by disenchanted members of the PDF in October 1989, the XVIII Airborne Corps became directly involved in the ongoing planning process for BLUE SPOON and participated directly in developing the OPORD 90-2 version of the plan. The strategic dimension of the plan was completely revised so that if offensive operations against the PDF took place, JTFSO would be established, JTF *Panama* would be dissolved, and JTF *Panama* staff and units would be placed under Stiner.[8] The revised OPLAN included a parachute assault at Omar-Torrijos International Airport, one of many changes intended to ensure that 27 PDF objectives could be simultaneously neutralized. On 18 December 1989, the national command authority directed the Joint Chiefs of Staff (JCS) to execute Operation Just Cause.[9]

The Chairman of the Joint Chiefs of Staff, in his execution order, stated U.S. goals for Operation Just Cause in three parts. The first set of goals included ensuring the freedom of transit through the Panama Canal, freedom from PDF abuse and harassment, and freedom to exercise U.S. treaty rights and responsibilities. The second set explicitly called for the removal of Noriega from power in Panama and the removal of his cronies and accomplices from office. And, finally, the JCS Chairman stated the constructive goals of creating both a PDF responsive to and supportive of an emergent democratic government in Panama and a freely elected and freely operating government of Panama (GOP).[10] These strategic objectives were then translated by the unified command into operational objectives, with the overall mission of neutralizing the PDF.

Planning was thus joint throughout, and occurred over an extended period of time. JTFSO's objectives in BLUE SPOON were to

- protect U.S. lives and key sites and facilities;
- capture and deliver Noriega to competent authority;
- neutralize PDF forces;
- neutralize PDF command and control;
- support establishment of a U.S.-recognized government in Panama; and
- restructure the PDF.[11]

---

[8] Yates, "Joint Task Force Panama," p. 69.

[9] *Operation Just Cause Lessons Learned*, Vol. 1, p. I-4.

[10] Message from Chairman, Joint Chiefs of Staff (CJCS), DTG 1823252Z, December 1989, Subject: Execute Order.

[11] *Operation Just Cause Lessons Learned*, Vol. 1, p. I-5.

For the most part, the planning for Operation Just Cause was admirable. It benefited from a long lead time before the actual operation, as well as U.S. officers' in-depth and close—frequently personal—knowledge of the PDF. It also benefited from lessons learned during the 1983 Operation Urgent Fury in Grenada, where joint operations were plagued by miscommunication between the services.[12] Without effective planning, the simultaneous attacks conducted on 27 locations would have been impossible. Planning also allowed maximum use of the airways (with different aircraft assigned to specific altitudes) and optimal coordination of each military service's capabilities and efforts.[13]

Yet the planning process demonstrated a larger problem of the overall effort: the lack of coordination between conventional operations and stability operations. Special operations and stability phase planning, rather than being considered as a package with conventional planning, were broken out and addressed separately,[14] with stability operations receiving the least attention and consideration despite their importance to the overall operation. Although planning is always compartmented in this way, the intention being to bring all the planners together in the last stages of the planning process, the division of planning responsibilities (and resources) in OJC served to deemphasize the postcombat-phase requirements despite their importance to the broader U.S. military mission. Ultimately, inattention to stability operations was detrimental to complementarity, timing, and coordination, resulting in some obvious failures, such as the dearth of civil affairs specialists available to meet post–D-day requirements and the communication problems during the stability phase of the operation between the Civil Military Operations Task Force (CMOTF) and the Joint Task Force *South* (JTFSO).

Force Structure

The U.S. force in Operation Just Cause totaled over 27,000, and included Air Force, Army, Navy, and Marine personnel in combat, combat support, and

---

[12]Planners for Operation Urgent Fury bypassed the 1979 Joint Deployment Agency (intended to coordinate rapid deployment forces) in favor of a Commander-in-Chief Atlantic (CINCLANT) planning group. The group was not successful in coordinating each service's contribution, and not only did a number of the special operations planned prove unrealistic and end disastrously, but U.S. aircraft accidentally attacked a U.S. brigade, and 10 of the 18 U.S. fatalities were due to accidents or friendly fire. White, *Swords of Lightning*, p. 256; Colonel Michael Dewar, *War in the Streets: The Story of Urban Combat from Calais to Khafji*, Brunel House: David & Charles, 1992, p. 80.

[13]Robert R. Ropelewski, "Planning, Precision, and Surprise Led to Panama Success," *Armed Forces Journal International*, February 1990, p. 28.

[14]The division of planning responsibilities is typical of military planning, not unique to Just Cause. A series of back briefs to coordinate the special operations and conventional planning then took place. Unfortunately, stability operations remained less of a priority, even in this process. Author's interviews at USSOCOM, May/June 1994.

combat service support roles. LTG Stiner, the commander in charge of all operations, controlled not only the Panama-based 193rd Infantry Brigade, but also most of the 7th Infantry Division, a brigade of the 82nd Airborne Division, one of the 5th Mechanized Division's battalions, all three of the Ranger regiment's battalions, the 7th Special Forces Group, a battalion-sized task force of SEALs, Special Boat Unit personnel from Naval Special Warfare Group-2, the 96th Civil Affairs Battalion, the 4th PSYOP Group, the 830th Air Division, the 24th Composite Wing from Howard Air Force Base, assets from the 1st Special Operations Wing of Hurlburt Field, Florida, the 41st Area Support Group, and the 112th Signal Brigade.[15]

This force mix was an unprecedented integration of light and heavy forces along with special operations forces, marking Operation Just Cause as a harbinger of the requirements of future U.S. contingency operations and demonstrating how far the military had come in executing joint operations since the problematic operation in Grenada six years earlier.

The force mix was made possible in part by the very limited PDF armor threat and made necessary by the need for military operations on urban terrain (MOUT), which call for light infantry (who clear and secure buildings and patrol) supported by mechanized infantry with mobile protected gun systems (providing shock effect and firepower for use in assaults, demonstrations, and gaining entry in walls and buildings).[16]

Special operations forces conducted combat operations during Operation Just Cause but were also involved in pre- and postcombat efforts. At H-hour, for example, members of Army Special Forces extracted American Kurt Frederick Muse from a prison in Panama. Another three Special Forces teams provided reconnaissance and surveillance against three critical sites and were responsible not only for watching the objectives but for interdicting any military forces leaving them.[17] After the operation, SOF language skills and regional expertise proved essential in the stability and later reconstruction operations.[18]

---

[15]U.S. Southern Command, *Command Briefing on Operation Just Cause*, p. 12; *Operation Just Cause: Joint Special Operations Task Force (JSOTF), OPORD 1-90 (Blue Spoon)*, Tampa, FL: MacDill Air Force Base, USSOCOM, January 1990. For more details on force structure, see the appendix.

[16]*Operation Just Cause Lessons Learned*, Vol. 2, "Operations," U.S. Army Combined Arms Command (CAC), Fort Leavenworth, KS: Center for Army Lessons Learned (CALL), No. 90-9, October 1990, p. II-2, II-3.

[17]Lieutenant Colonel William C. Bennett, "Just Cause and the Principles of War," *Military Review*, March 1991, p. 9.

[18]Special operations forces used their language and cultural skills to facilitate communication between U.S. conventional forces and the Panamanian public. They were also heavily involved in the early efforts to train a new Panamanian police force and contributed to rebuilding Panama's government and judiciary.

It is likely that future U.S. operations will have force structures similar to the one employed in Panama. Even in Operation Desert Storm (ODS)—a much grander, battlefield war—forces from all four services worked together and with special operators to coordinate their planning and actions. OJC's mix of light and heavy infantry is also likely to be replicated in future OOTW, which will probably take place in heavily populated urban environments requiring the flexibility and maneuverability of light forces alongside mechanized units' ability to breach buildings and walls and apply massive firepower when necessary. Special operations forces and military police trained in peacetime ROE will also be as valuable in future OOTW as they were in OJC, perhaps more valuable. SOF's cultural and language skills, as well as their utility as combat multipliers, will remain in demand, as will MPs' special police training and ability to deal with civilians.

Coordination Between the Players

Thanks to effective planning, coordination between all participants in Operation Just Cause was exemplary. A clear chain of command existed from the President to the Commander-in-Chief (CINC). Moreover, because General Thurman gave Lieutenant General Stiner operational control of the entire fighting force, the chain of command remained clearly delineated down to the tactical level.[19] Even when subordinate units had their higher headquarters change in the course of the conflict, the passage of operational control was clearly delineated and stated in appropriate fragmentary orders.[20] Stiner himself, in testimony before the Senate Armed Services Committee, gave credit to the 1986 Goldwater-Nichols Department of Defense Reorganization Act for ensuring that "there were no problems with ambiguous relationships or units receiving guidance from multiple sources."[21]

Because of the heavy reliance on special operations forces, coordination between them and conventional forces was critical. Some military personnel argue that such coordination was compromised because the Civil Military Operations Task Force (CMOTF)[22] reported directly to SOUTHCOM J5 rather than to LTG Stiner,

---

[19]Bennett, "Just Cause and the Principles of War," p. 6.

[20]Ibid., p. 9.

[21]Lieutenant General Stiner's response to the chairman, Senate Armed Services Committee, prehearing defense policy questions, dated 11 May 1990.

[22]Between 26 December 1989 and 1 January 1990, the CMOTF consisted of 25 reserve volunteers with no cohesive organization and no authority over military police forces. By mid-January, when it was brought under the control of the newly established Military Support Group (MSG) under JTFSO, the CMOTF still had only 140 personnel and no command or control over military police. The SOUTHCOM J3 recommended, and USCINCSO directed, that military police forces would remain under JTFSO (then JTF *Panama*) rather than the CMOTF or the MSG. It was this decision that led to

and had no control over military police forces.[23] These critics credit the disjuncture between the CMOTF and JTFSO for leading to the breakdown of public security following the U.S. invasion and for being partially responsible for the destructive looting and violence in Panama City.[24] Yet this assessment is not universally shared. Other military personnel suggest that the breakdown in public security had nothing to do with the CMOTF and JTFSO relationship, but was actually due to the fact that the 82nd Airborne could not fulfill its mission as planned (which would have involved its presence in the city) because it got bogged down during the combat airdrop.[25] Still others point out that the anarchic situation in the city was not only unanticipated, but could not be a U.S. priority as long as U.S. forces were still tracking down Noriega and other PDF leaders.[26]

Regardless of the situation between the CMOTF and JTFSO, SOF and conventional infantry were generally able to leverage off each other and maximize their combined capabilities by cooperating in operational elements functioning as quick reaction forces. Because of their language and cultural training, special operations forces also served effectively as liaisons between conventional force area commanders and the local civilian government and police officials. Finally, the U.S. Army special forces were critical in conducting the preliminary medical and engineer assessments and surveys that helped establish the baseline civil-military operation plan.[27] Such successes were all the more telling because Just Cause incorporated an unprecedented number of SOF capabilities; indeed, the operation represented the first major deployment of SOF forces after the establishment of the U.S. Special Operations Command (USSOCOM).[28]

---

the above-mentioned criticism. COL Harold W. Youmans, memorandum to author, Tampa, FL: MacDill Air Force Base, USSOCOM, 10 March 1994.

[23]Indeed, problems associated with SOUTHCOM's control of the CMOTF led to the eventual creation during Operation Promote Liberty of the Military Support Group (MSG) under the JTFSO, comprising a special forces task force (JSOTF), a PSYOP task force (JPOTF), and a civil affairs task force (CMOTF).

[24]John T. Fishel, "The Murky World of Conflict Termination: Planning and Executing the 1989–90 Restoration of Panama," *Small Wars and Insurgencies*, Vol. 3, No. 1, Spring 1992, pp. 62–64. Discussions with MAJ Richard D. Downie, Santa Monica, California, Spring 1992.

[25]Colonel Glenn A. Brazelton, USAF, interview with author, Tampa, FL: USSOCOM, 31 May 1994. Colonel Brazelton was on the SOUTHCOM J3 staff during OJC.

[26]COL Paul Morgan, USA (ret.), interview with author, Tampa, FL: USSOCOM, 31 May 1994; Youmans memorandum to author.

[27]*Operation Just Cause Lessons Learned*, Vol. 2, p. II-4. Special forces conducted similar preliminary survey and assessment functions in Operation Sea Angel, where their work helped direct emergency assistance and supplies. Special forces also served as liaisons between the U.S. military, local government and military officials, and nongovernmental organizations providing humanitarian assistance in the area.

[28]Ibid.

Because of the nature of the conflict, operations were extremely decentralized and executed at the platoon and squad level. This meant that the commanders' intent had to be extremely clear and that junior leaders had to be trained and prepared to take the initiative when necessary. This was very successful in Operation Just Cause, where prior leadership training and reinforcement of initiative proved invaluable.[29]

Liaison officers (LNOs) assigned to specific units (dedicated liaison officers) also contributed to streamlining command and control, although there were not enough of them and they had not been integrated into training exercises and combat training centers (CTCs) prior to the operation. LNOs were especially helpful when, as sometimes occurred, standard operating procedures (SOPs) were not followed and communications networks became overloaded. It was also evident that infantry brigades with MP companies attached to them during the stability operations needed a military police (MP) LNO.[30]

Training

Because the situation in Panama eroded over a relatively prolonged period, U.S. forces had the opportunity to train specifically for operations there. JTF *Panama*, for example, ran a series of joint training exercises throughout the summer and fall of 1989. Known as PURPLE STORMs and SAND FLEAs, these exercises allowed U.S. troops to practice components of BLUE SPOON. Troops also participated in combat readiness exercises (CREs) to improve the speed with which they could begin operations. In the weeks prior to Operation Just Cause, the Panama-based 193rd Infantry Brigade maintained a seven-days-a-week training schedule and conducted a month of live-fire operations in a simulated urban environment, advancing from squad- to platoon-level operations. They also familiarized themselves with the roads leading to many key facilities and the plans to secure and protect them. The 5-87th C-Company ran a practice offensive against an "enemy" camp.[31] JTFSO's conventional airborne forces and the JSOTF also had the opportunity to rehearse their components of the offensive OPORD directly prior to Operation Just Cause.[32]

---

[29]Ibid., p. II-5.

[30]Ibid., Vol. 2, pp. II-19, II-20. MP advisors could also be attached to each company simply to provide their expertise in dealing with civilians and searching buildings. Major Robert G. Boyko, "Just Cause: MOUT Lessons Learned," *Infantry*, May–June 1991.

[31]Donna Miles, "Training to Fight," *Soldiers*, February 1990, pp. 37–43; *Operation Just Cause Lessons Learned*, Vol. 2, p. II-4.

[32]All the exercises exacerbated tension between the two countries and were widely criticized in the Panamanian press, which warned of an impending U.S. invasion. U.S. Southern Command, *Command Briefing on Operation Just Cause*, pp. 6–9; David A. Fulghum, "Army Tells Congress That Aviators Rehearsed U.S. Invasion of Panama," *Aviation Week and Space Technology*, 11 June 1990, p. 23.

Some of the troops participating in OJC also benefited from participation in the post-Grenada "No Notice" training exercises—such as the 1988 GOLDEN PHEASANT exercise in Honduras—that helped improve American capabilities in operations other than war.[33]

These rehearsals and simulations in MOUT and OOTW tactics and techniques were particularly valuable given that most U.S. military training (Army basic and advanced infantry training, for example) focuses on the application of maximum force. Because MOUT appears in very few units' mission essential task lists (METLs), it is frequently an afterthought in training.[34] Even Army light infantry units—the units formed principally for operations other than war and likely to carry most of the burden of MOUT in future OOTW—receive most of their training in conventional, battlefield warfare. All such units would benefit from training in the basics of MOUT and OOTW, including patrolling, ambushes, roadblocks, cordon and search operations, building clearing, riot control, and protection of key facilities. Even in Panama, where the forces functioned well, U.S. military efforts would have been more efficient and less destructive had the forces been trained in such skills.[35]

As mentioned earlier, allowing small unit leaders—including junior NCOs—to take the initiative proved extremely successful in Panama. Encouraging initiative and providing leadership training at the lowest levels is critical in MOUT and OOTW, given the decentralization of operations in such conflict environments. As demonstrated in Panama, training junior officers as well as training at the unit level, including live-fire exercises at crew, team, squad, section and platoon level, is extremely valuable preparation for operations other than war.[36]

Intelligence

Intelligence was not sufficiently collected, managed, and disseminated during Operation Just Cause. One problem was that area specialists were not

---

[33]White, *Swords of Lightning*, p. 260.

[34]MOUT training has improved since Operation Just Cause, although many units still do not receive it. Both the Army and the Marines have adjusted some of their MOUT exercises and training to reflect MOUT in OOTW as opposed to MOUT in battlefield warfare (where the presence of civilians is not anticipated and infrastructural damage does not have to be avoided). Melissa Healy, "Army Emphasizes Urban Warfare Training in Wake of Panama Invasion," *Los Angeles Times*, 17 February 1990, p. 26; "Tale of Two Courses," *Soldier of Fortune*, April 1990, p. 96; Owen Moritz, "Pentagon Plans Training Camp for Art of Urban Warfare," *New York Daily News*, 15 February 1990, p. 6; Dewar, *War in the Streets*, p. 78.

[35]See the following section on MOUT for a more specific discussion of how MOUT training would have benefited U.S. forces. For an excellent discussion of the requirements of MOUT and the need for improved training, see Steven N. Collins, "*Just Cause* Up Close: A Light Infantryman's View of LIC," *Parameters*, Summer 1992; Boyko, "Just Cause: MOUT Lessons Learned."

[36]*Operation Just Cause Lessons Learned*, Vol. 1, p. I-18.

Military Operations on Urban Terrain

MOUT requires very different skills and capabilities than does warfare on open terrain. City lights, high-rise buildings, and dense civilian populations (possibly in flight), represent unique obstacles and challenges. Light infantry, because of their ability to patrol, clear buildings, scout, and provide target reference points, play a larger role in MOUT than mechanized forces, but they nonetheless require mechanized support. Precision weapons, light antitank weapons (LAW), and mortars and field artillery allow more surgical attacks and limit civilian casualties and collateral damage.

Snipers are ideal assets in urban settings. They allow greater precision and efficiency, and are an excellent force multiplier. A single sniper can effectively slow, or even direct, opposing forces' movements.

The nonlinear front in MOUT has repercussions for force protection, especially combat service support and combat support units. These units, which in battlefield warfare enjoy the relative security of maintaining the rear, require additional protection or defensive capabilities in MOUT warfare, where there is no front and the enemy can emerge from anywhere.

The nonlinear front and limited access to the combat area also have implications for medical response. Hospitals or medical facilities, in the absence of a defined front (which allows them to remain relatively secure in the rear), must be located far from the amorphous combat area. Moreover, tall buildings, snipers, booby traps, and anti-aircraft capabilities inhibit evacuation by ground or by helicopter. Units must therefore be prepared to provide their own medical attention in case of casualties. Some training along these lines is already available in the Army through the combat lifesaving program. Because there are far too few medics (approximately one medic per 50 soldiers in the Army) to cover dispersed combat areas, some personnel in each unit receive training as combat lifesavers. These troops are less skilled than medics, but they can help keep their comrades alive until they reach hospitals. The proportion of combat lifesavers per unit is not consistent (at the battalion level it ranges from approximately 10 to 25 percent) and depends on the unit leader's support for such training.[56]

In urban operations other than war, sufficient troops must be available to control refugees and keep the roads clear without diverting combat power, and combat

---

[56]One Army multiple-launch rocket system (MLRS) battalion's goal is to train fully 50 percent of the soldiers in combat lifesaving, so that there is at least one combat lifesaver for each launcher. The battalion commander's rationale is that in conventional warfare, launchers disperse and medics will not be readily available. The same problem with dispersal, of course, holds true for almost any unit operating in MOOTW or MOUT.

service support must be sufficiently stocked to provide food, clothing, shelter, and medical attention to refugees.[57] Such concerns usually do not apply to conventional, battlefield warfare, where civilians are assumed to have been evacuated and the welfare of those remaining is not the responsibility of the invading force.

MOUT also requires special equipment and knowledge about the effects of certain ammunition, weapons, and devices. U.S. forces operating in Panama City quickly learned that they had to be careful which weapons they applied. For their own and civilian safety, for example, they needed to be aware of how buildings' interior construction would hold up to different weapons' fire, grenades, and explosive charges. Because of the need to carry their own equipment, often up and down stairways, at a run through streets, or through narrow alleyways, light, collapsible weapons proved more useful than bulky weapons. Also, because of the likelihood of close combat in heavily populated areas, accuracy and speed were important characteristics of any weapon system or equipment. Troops also needed the capability to punch holes in walls and breach fences, concertina wire, and iron bars.

In OJC, MOUT efforts were complicated by some unanticipated requirements. For example, fire control and identification, friend or foe (IFF) proved very difficult in the city. Military maps did not adequately identify buildings. Sufficient presence was not maintained in the city, allowing looting and violence to occur. Units had to divert resources and personnel in order to control and safeguard refugees. Building clearing also proved to be more manpower intensive than foreseen, diverting yet more resources and combat power. Finally, troops were not always appropriately prepared or armed. The night-vision goggles and M44 night sights on the M551 were susceptible to city lights, soldiers lacked simple but necessary equipment like flashlights and wirecutters, and the guns and mortars with which they deployed were not always appropriate.[58] The tactical difficulties in Panama City demonstrated how much conventional MOUT practitioners and planners could learn about equipment and tactics from special operations forces and civilian police special weapons and tactics (SWAT) units, both of which are specially trained in urban operations, the nonlethal application of force, and in breaching and entering fortified urban locations.

---

[57]Captain John S. Zachau, "Military Operations on Urban Terrain," *Infantry*, November–December 1992, pp. 44–46.

[58]In subsequent analyses, the U.S. Army Center for Lessons Learned (CALL) determined that ideal weapons for MOUT include the M-2 .50-caliber heavy barrel machine gun, the 90-mm recoilless rifle, LAW, the M-9 bayonet, and simpler technologies like flashlights, wirecutters, and shotguns. *Operation Just Cause Lessons Learned*, Vol. 2, p. II-11, II-12.

invasion. In the future, U.S. planners will have to anticipate such destructive behavior by opposition forces, and U.S. forces must be prepared to respond to— or even prevent—arson, looting, and riots.

Stability Operations

The transition from combat operations to the stability phase of Operation Just Cause was one of the most problematic aspects of the operation. As areas were cleared of the PDF, in both the cities and the countryside, immediate requirements arose for assistance to the local populations. Yet, for a number of reasons, the transition was not smooth. First, as discussed above, the stability phase received insufficient attention during the planning stages of the operation. Indeed, while the combat phase of the operation was planned down to the last detail, troops entering the stability phase were frequently left to their own devices and had to respond ad hoc to the demands of the local population. This situation was further exacerbated by the fact that there was no presidential call-up for reserve forces, where 96 percent of the U.S. Army civil affairs and roughly two-thirds of the psychological operations personnel reside.[67] Furthermore, because civilians had not been involved in the planning of Operation Just Cause for reasons of operational security, neither the State Department nor any other U.S. civilian agency was sufficiently prepared to assume responsibility for postcombat nation-building programs.[68]

Thus, toward the end of the combat phase of the operation, before adequate civil affairs personnel had arrived and while MPs were still conducting battlefield missions,[69] combat units were thrust into situations where they were responsible

---

[67]The only civil affairs personnel to arrive in Panama after the 20 December deployment of the 96th Civil Affairs Battalion were volunteers. Similar problems plagued Operation Desert Storm (where the presidential call-up took place relatively late in the operation) and Operation Restore Hope (where no call-up took place, and volunteers were again the supplement to the 96th Civil Affairs Battalion).

[68]DoD officials excluded civilian agencies from the planning process by classifying all PRAYER BOOK plans, which included both the BLUE SPOON warfighting plan and the civil-military and stability operations plan BLIND LOGIC. All plans were held exclusively within JCS channels. Postconflict planning responsibilities thus fell to military personnel unfamiliar with the requirements of the process, even though it was recognized from the outset that the effective implementation of the postconflict plan required prior coordination with civil U.S. agencies, especially the State Department. DoD officials further handicapped postconflict planning by limiting the resources for the process and—in an unconventional move reflecting the low priority they gave to postconflict activities—assigning to a planning staff responsibility for executing the postconflict operations.

[69]Critics of the operation charge that there were some costly failures during the stability phase, and point to the late activation of U.S. military police in Panama City, which, they claim, left room for the destructive looting and violence that took place. Author's interview with an anonymous Army lieutenant colonel, 8 August 1991; "Army Force Structure Overhaul Incomplete, Problems Remain: GAO," *Aerospace Daily*, 4 December 1990, pp. 374–375; Yates, "Joint Task Force Panama," p. 71.

for stability operations for which they were neither trained nor prepared.[70] They had to fulfill such diverse responsibilities as traffic control, garbage collection, establishing law and order, and providing food, water, and health care to the local population.[71] These units were eventually supported by civil affairs, medical personnel, special forces, MPs, and engineers, but only well into the stability phase of the operation.[72]

Postconflict Military Operations

Upon completion of Operation Just Cause, a follow-on operation, Operation Promote Liberty, was begun. In that operation, U.S. efforts focused on rebuilding Panama's institutional infrastructure. Civil affairs, PSYOP, MP, special forces, engineering and logistical personnel all cooperated in this effort. Yet a certain amount of confusion arose during the operation over responsibilities for civil-military and stability operations. For example, because establishing a new Panamanian police force was a priority for the United States, within days after the combat operation, LTG Stiner set up the U.S. Forces Liaison Group (USFLG) in the headquarters of the Panama National Police, under the direct command of MG Marc A. Cisneros, Commander, U.S. Army South (USARSO). The USFLG was created to help reconfigure Panama's police. Most of the USFLG officers were foreign area specialists (FAOs), and most of the U.S. personnel in the office were fluent in Spanish. At the end of January 1990, when the Civil Military Operations Task Force, the Joint Special Operations Task Force (a new JSOTF), and the Joint Psychological Operations Task Force (JPOTF) were placed under the newly established Military Support Group (MSG) under JTFSO,[73] the USFLG was subordinated to the MSG and renamed the Public Force Liaison Division (PFLD). The new MSG became responsible for all civil-military relations with the new government. In February, JTFSO was deactivated, and the MSG came under the control of the reactivated JTF *Panama* under USARSO Commander Cisneros.[74]

---

[70]MAJ Thomas C. Maffey, USA, interview with author, Tampa, FL: USSOCOM, 1 June 1994. General Thurman defended the mix of combat and civil affairs personnel, pointing out that during Operation Just Cause, U.S. troops occupied 142 sites in a conscious effort to protect the public utilities of the city. Moore and Tyler, "U.S. Paratroopers May Have Seen Noriega Escape During Invasion," p. A22.

[71]Mark A. Uhlig, "In Rural Panama, Hard Questions Remain About Who's in Charge," *The New York Times*, 12 January 1990, p. A16.

[72]For more on the role of MPs in Operation Just Cause, including their critical force-protection function, see Colonel Robert B. Killebrew, "Force Projection in Short Wars," *Military Review*, March 1991, pp. 19–27, and Donna Miles, "MPs Were Ready," *Soldiers*, February 1990, pp. 41–43.

[73]The CMOTF was placed under the MSG along with the Joint PSYOP Task Force and the Joint Special Operations Task Force, made up of the remaining TF *Black* troops.

[74]U.S. Special Operations Command briefing, *Formation of U.S. Military Support Group for Operation Promote Liberty*, January 1990; John T. Fishel, *The Fog of Peace: Planning and Executing the*

- In most OOTW the battlefield is nonlinear, and units may be dispersed in cities or over a vast area, as in Somalia. Small units must be therefore be more self-sufficient.

Accordingly, standard leadership training and reinforcement of initiative extended to younger officers and small-unit leaders should continue. Training in special skills that increase the flexibility of small units should also be undertaken. The combat lifesaver program, for example, increases a unit's survivability without increasing its total personnel.

Intelligence

- Electronic intelligence (ELINT) is not well suited to OOTW. HUMINT is required, but it will not be sufficient to meet commanders' needs. Coordination between the military and the CIA can supplement HUMINT, but such cooperation was lacking in Just Cause.

Accordingly, military personnel must exhaust all HUMINT possibilities, including NGOs/HROs and military-to-military contacts. Coordination of intelligence collection and information dissemination between the military and the intelligence community must also be a priority. While such coordination was still inadequate during Operation Desert Storm, it had improved somewhat by the time of Operation Restore Hope in Somalia. Finally, HUMINT and ELINT should be supplemented by SIGINT and IMINT.

- Joint attempts to streamline intelligence led information to be too general.

Accordingly, units' intelligence requirements must be made known to, and understood by, collection managers at higher headquarters.

Equipment

- OJC clearly demonstrated MOUT's special equipment requirements. Simple technologies such as wirecutters, flashlights, and appropriate rifles would have benefited soldiers tremendously. More sophisticated technologies such as NVGs and flash-bang grenades were not specifically designed for MOUT, and required adjustment for that terrain. Also, weapons allowing direct fire and surgical strikes are more critical than those designed for indirect fire.

Lessons learned during OJC about the value of rifles, light packs, NVGs, and other equipment and weaponry suitable to operations on urban terrain have already been incorporated into some Army doctrine (see the most recent FM 90-10-1) and research and development. NVGs, for example, have been adjusted to cope with city lights. Other advancements in technology applicable to OOTW have also been made since 1989.[2] The real question for OOTW, however, is not what kinds of technology are required, but whether relatively simple technologies (even such things as wirecutters and riot-control gear) are available in sufficient amounts. U.S. military procurement processes tend to make access to simple equipment expensive and slow, especially when others can simply buy comparable equipment over the counter.

Postcombat Operations

- The military, concerned about operational secrecy, gave civilian agencies little warning about the need for their support in postcombat operations. This slowed and complicated the transition from military to civilian operations following the combat phase of Operation Just Cause.

Accordingly, where possible, the military must include representatives from civilian governmental organizations as well as NGOs/HROs in the planning process. Where operational secrecy truly precludes such civilian involvement, the military must ensure that postcombat operations are not only sufficiently funded and resourced, but that knowledgeable and experienced people are included in the planning teams. Liaisons to military planning groups from civilian agencies and organizations could help ensure that military planning takes into account civilian strengths and constraints from the outset.

- Civilian agencies were unprepared to salvage the situation once they were apprised of the need for their assistance in postcombat operations.

Accordingly, civilian agencies (including the State Department, Justice Department, and the U.S. Agency for International Development) must not only be involved in the planning for most OOTW, but must develop the capabilities and standard operating procedures to offer valuable and timely contributions. Such postconflict requirements as setting up U.S. country teams; coordinating U.S. civilian and military efforts; establishing and organizing civilian agencies; training civilian administrators and, perhaps, police; assisting in the demobilization of militaries; and building infrastructure may devolve to U.S.

---

[2]Edward Bedrosian et al., *Technology for Low Intensity Conflict*, Santa Monica, CA: RAND, MR-421-ARPA/OSD, 1994.

civilian agencies following future OOTW, and the agencies must be better prepared than they were for OJC.

Conclusion

Many future conflicts will be characterized by urban combat, civilian presence, and humanitarian requirements. For the U.S. armed forces, and the Army in particular, this will require changes in how combat is undertaken. The tactics and techniques that are most effective in conventional battlefield warfare do not necessarily apply to OOTW. Training, doctrine, and equipment will have to be adjusted to accommodate OOTW requirements. These efforts can be informed, in part, by Operation Just Cause; though somewhat different than later OOTW in Bangladesh, Bosnia, Somalia, Rwanda, and Haiti, this operation nonetheless yields some valuable lessons for combat, combat support, and combat service support units engaged in urban operations other than war.

Appendix
Task Force Organization

Task Force Bayonet
193 INF BDE
5-87 INF
1-508 INF
4-6 MECH

Task Force Atlantic
HQ 7 INF DIV
2D BDE
3D BDE

Task Force Pacific
HQ 82 ABN DIV
1ST BDE, 82D
CO/3-73 AR
BTTY/1-319 FA
1-4 POG (9xHB TMS)
9TH INF REGT
20xUH-60
4xAH-1
2xOH-58

Task Force Semper Fidelis
MARFOR-PM
LT AR INF CO
RIFLE CO

Task Force White
NSWTG-2 (SEALS)
ST-4 (4xSEAL PLT)
NSWU-8
    SBU-26 (3xPB)
    SEAL PLT-FWD (1xPLT)
1723 CCS (CCT)
1-4 POG (1xHB TM)
1xAC-130 (DS)

NOTE: Because of the author's reliance on various sources, this listing is not completely consistent in the level of detail provided for each task force. While some are defined down to the company and platoon levels, others are listed at higher aggregates. The sources are U.S. Southern Command, *Command Briefing on Operation Just Cause*, pp. 16–21; Miles, "Panama: Operation Just Cause," pp. 22–24; U.S. Special Operations Command briefing, *Operation Just Cause*, January 1990; and U.S. Special Operations Command briefing, *Operation Just Cause: Joint Special Operations Task Force (JSOTF)*, January 1990.

Task Force Black
SOCSOUTH
3/7 SFG (-)
A/1/7 SFG
DET 1-4 POG (1xHB TM)
DET 1723 CCS (CCT)
2xAC-130 (DS)
617 SOAD (5xMH-60)

Task Force Red-Romeo
75 RGR REGT (-)
2-75 RGR
3-75 RGR
DET 1724 STSQ (CCT/PJ)
DET 1-4 POG (3xHB TMS)
1xAC130 (DS)
2xF117

Task Force Red-Tango
1-75 RGR (+)
C/3-75 RGR
DET 1-4 POG (3xHB TMS)
DET 96 CAB (3xCA TMS)
DET 1724 STSQ (CCT/PJ)
1xAC-130 (DS)
2xAH-6 (DS)

Task Force Green
USA SMU

Task Force Blue
USN SMU

Task Force Gator
4-6 MECH (-)
CO/1-508 INF
PLT/3-73 AR
PLT/LT AR INF (LAV)
CO/504 MP
DET 1724 STSQ (CCT)
DET 1-4 POG (1xHB TM)

1ST Special Operations Wing (SOW)

160 Special Operations Aviation Group (SOAG)

Tactical Air Command (TAC)

Bibliography

"AH-64s Valued in Panama Operation: Night Vision Proved Very Valuable," *Helicopter News*, 26 January 1990.

"Airlift Activity," *Aerospace Daily*, 4 September 1990.

"Army Force Structure Overhaul Incomplete, Problems Remain: GAO," *Aerospace Daily*, 4 December 1990.

Aswell, P. L., *Wartime Press Censorship by the U.S. Armed Forces: A Historical Perspective*, Master's Thesis, Fort Leavenworth, KS: U.S. Army Command and General Staff College, 1990.

Baker, James, U.S. Secretary of State, excerpted speech, 20 December 1989, *Latin American Weekly Report*, WR-90-1, 11 January 1990.

Bedrosian, Edward, et al., *Technology for Low Intensity Conflict*, Santa Monica, CA: RAND, MR-421-ARPA/OSD, 1994.

Bennett, Lieutenant Colonel William C., "Just Cause and the Principles of War," *Military Review*, March 1991.

Boyko, Major Robert G., "Just Cause: MOUT Lessons Learned," *Infantry*, May–June 1991.

Buckley, Kevin, *Panama: The Whole Story*, New York: Simon and Schuster, 1991.

Capaccio, Tony, "Apache Worked as Advertised in Panama Operations," *Defense Week*, 22 January 1990.

"Changed NVG Policies, Procedures Boost Safety, Army Says," *Aerospace Daily*, 8 June 1990.

Collins, Steven N., "*Just Cause* Up Close: A Light Infantryman's View of LIC," *Parameters*, Summer 1992.

Crichton, J. E., *Department of Defense Press Pool: Did It Work in Panama*, Master's Thesis, Tucson, AZ: The University of Arizona, 1990.

Cuddihee, Lieutenant Colonel Michael A., and Schmidt, Lieutenant Colonel John W., *Special Operations Forces: Responsive, Capable, and Ready*, Maxwell Air Force Base, AL: Air University, 1990.

Devroy, Ann, "U.S. Keeps Troops on Sidelines," *Washington Post*, 4 October 1989.

Dewar, Colonel Michael, *War in the Streets: The Story of Urban Combat from Calais to Khafji*, Brunel House: David & Charles, 1992.

Downie, Major Richard, "Taking Responsibility for Our Actions?" unpublished paper, 1991.

Erlanger, Steven, "U.S. Economic Warfare Brings Disaster to Panama," *The New York Times*, 9 June 1988.

Fishel, John T., "The Murky World of Conflict Termination: Planning and Executing the 1989–90 Restoration of Panama," *Small Wars and Insurgencies*, Vol. 3, No. 1, Spring 1992.

Fulghum, David A., "Army Tells Congress that Aviators Rehearsed U.S. Invasion of Panama," *Aviation Week and Space Technology*, 11 June 1990.

Gerstenzang, James, "Bush Urges Coup to Topple Noriega," *Los Angeles Times*, 14 May 1989.

Gerstenzang, James, and John M. Broder, "Step Down, Bush Urges Noriega," *Los Angeles Times*, 10 May 1989.

"Getting SEALs Ashore," *Jane's Defence Weekly*, 12 May 1990.

Gruson, Lindsay, "Carter Says Soldiers Seize Tallies and Block Counting of Vote in Panama," *The New York Times*, 8 May 1989.

Halloran, Richard, "U.S. Troops to Go Slowly Into Panama," *The New York Times*, 12 May 1989.

Healy, Melissa, "Army Emphasizes Urban Warfare Training in Wake of Panama Invasion," *Los Angeles Times*, 17 February 1990.

Hughes, David, "Night Airdrop in Panama Surprises Noriega's Forces," *Aviation Week and Space Technology*, 1 January 1990.

Killebrew, Colonel Robert B., "Force Projection in Short Wars," *Military Review*, March 1991.

Labrut, Michele, "U.S. Facilities Stoned in Panama," *Miami Herald*, 1 July 1987.

Lauter, David, "U.S. Breaks Off Relations With Panama," *Los Angeles Times*, 2 September 1989.

Lopez, Ramon, "US Army Learns Panama Lessons," *Jane's Defence Weekly*, 12 May 1990.

McManus, Doyle, "Noriega Move to End Panama Crisis Reported," *Los Angeles Times*, 5 August 1988.

Message from Chairman, Joint Chiefs of Staff (CJCS), DTG 1823252Z, December 1989, Subject: Execute Order.

Miles, Donna, "MPs Were Ready," *Soldiers*, February 1990.

————, "Training to Fight," *Soldiers*, February 1990, pp. 37–43;

————, "Panama: Operation Just Cause," *Soldiers*, February 1990.

Moore, Molly, and Patrick E. Tyler, "U.S. Paratroopers May Have Seen Noriega Escape During Invasion," *Washington Post*, 7 January 1990.

Moritz, Owen, "Pentagon Plans Training Camp For Art of Urban Warfare," *New York Daily News*, 15 February 1990.

Operation Just Cause Lessons Learned, Vol. 1, "Soldiers and Leadership," Fort Leavenworth, KS: Center for Army Lessons Learned (CALL), U.S. Army Combined Arms Command (CAC), October 1990.

Operation Just Cause Lessons Learned, Vol. 2, "Operations," Fort Leavenworth, KS: Center for Army Lessons Learned (CALL), U.S. Army Combined Arms Command (CAC), No. 90-9, October 1990.

Operation Just Cause Lessons Learned, Vol. 3, "Intelligence, Logistics, and Equipment," Fort Leavenworth, KS: Center for Army Lessons Learned (CALL), U.S. Army Combined Arms Command (CAC), No. 90-9, October 1990.

Ottoway, David B., "Pentagon Aide Reportedly Pressures Noriega to Resign," *Los Angeles Times*, 8 January 1988.

"Panama Invasion Takes Chopper Toll: Special Operation Damage Is Heavy," *Helicopter News*, 12 January 1990.

"Panama Lessons Spur Call to Fit A-130 with Hellfire, Other Upgrades," *Aerospace Daily*, 17 October 1990.

"Panama's Testing Ground," *Jane's Defence Weekly*, 12 May 1990.

Pear, Robert, "Military Arrests Exacerbate U.S.-Panamanian Relations," *The New York Times*, 8 October 1989.

Preston, Major Joseph W., "Just Cause: Intelligence Support to Special Operations Aviation," *Military Intelligence*, July–September 1990.

Risk Assessment Monthly, Vol. 10, No. 3, March 1988.

Risk Assessment Weekly, Vol. 5, No. 11, 18 March 1988.

Ropelewski, Robert R., "Planning, Precision, and Surprise Led to Panama Success," *Armed Forces Journal International*, February 1990.

Ropp, Steven C., "Panama's Defiant Noriega," *Current History*, December 1988.

Schultz, Richard H., Jr., *The Post-Conflict Use of Military Forces: Lessons from Panama*, International Security Studies Program, Tufts University, 1991.

Sciolino, Elaine, "U.S. Is Considering Action on Panama," *The New York Times*, 9 January 1988.

Scranton, Margaret E., "Panama," in Peter J. Schraeder (ed.), *Intervention into the 1990s: U.S Foreign Policy in the Third World*, second edition, Boulder, CO: Lynne Rienner Publishers, 1992.

Shannon, Don, and Kenneth Freed, "Noriega Again Thwarts U.S. Ouster," *Los Angeles Times*, 1 September 1989.

Smolowe, Jill, "The Yanquis Stayed Home," *Time*, 16 October 1989.

"Some Question Whether the U.S. Is Ready for LIC," *Navy News and Undersea Technology*, 27 August 1990.

"Statistics Corner," *Aerospace Daily*, 24 September 1990.

Stiner, Lieutenant General Carl W., response to the chairman, Senate Armed Services Committee, prehearing defense policy questions, 11 May 1990.

"Tale of Two Courses," *Soldier of Fortune*, April 1990, p. 96.

"TF-160 in Panama," *Helicopter International*, April 1990.

"Tighter Panama Sanctions," *Los Angeles Times*, 13 September 1989.

Uhlig, Mark A., "In Rural Panama, Hard Questions Remain About Who's in Charge," *The New York Times*, 12 January 1990.

U.S. Southern Command, *Command Briefing on Operation Just Cause*, no date.

"US Troops Pull Back," *Latin American Weekly Report*, 3 May 1990.

Vallance-Whitacre, J. R., *An Evaluation of the Media Coverage Concerning the Mission to Secure the Dog Kennel During the Panama Invasion on December 20, 1989*, Master's Thesis, Richmond, VA: Virginia Commonwealth University, 1990.

"Welch Didn't Want F-117s Sent to Panama, But Had No Alternative," *Aerospace Daily*, 12 June 1990.

White, Terry, *Swords of Lightning: Special Forces and the Changing Face of Warfare*, London: Brassey's (UK), 1992.

Wilson, George C., "SouthCom Commander Rewrote Contingency Plans for Action," *Washington Post*, 7 January 1990.

Wines, Michael, "U.S. Plans New Effort to Oust Noriega," *The New York Times*, 17 November 1989.

Wood, Major Samuel S., Jr., "Joint Fire Support in Low Intensity Conflict," *Military Review*, March 1991.

Wright, Robin, "U.S. in New Bid to Oust Noriega," *Los Angeles Times*, 16 November 1989.

Yates, Lawrence A., "Joint Task Force Panama: JUST CAUSE—Before and After," *Military Review*, October 1991.

Zachau, John S., Captain, "Military Operations on Urban Terrain," *Infantry*, November–December 1992, pp. 44–46.